COLOR

This book's purpose is to provide gorgeous displays of handmade products therein. It is sold with the understanding that you will enjoy the photos. If you don't enjoy them, then you should probably eat a cupcake or two and ride a unicorn.

Publisher: Renae Christine
Editor: Jackie Rapetti
Editor: Renae Christine
Assistant Editor: Rebecca Cote
Author: Carey Bunker
Art Director: Carey Bunker
Design Assistant: Galilee Anne Morallos
Photographer: By Hello Charlie; Emily Butterworth and Megan Donnenwerth
Production Assistant: Tom Cote
Cover Design: Aubrey Hill

Written in the United States of America
10 9 8 7 6 5 4 3 2 1

Dedicated to all who are color-obsessed
as if it were a welcome disease.

All featured handmade products
in *Color* were sponsored
by Renae Christine's amazing Besties
(aka Renae's YouTube followers).

Pair *Color* with homemade dinner rolls and
raspberry jam whilst perusing.

WHY COLOR EXISTS

The existence of color seeps into art classes, photographs and TV.

But if you obsess over colors like I do, you know color has a much greater importance than the color of shoes you recently purchased. By the way they look fantastic on you, *wink.

We pretend not to obsess over color because it almost seems childish. What if someone thinks I'm shallow? What if someone rolls their eyes when I'm staring a little too long at that Thomas Kinkade Christmas puzzle I just finished?

Psychologically, we can't help it.

We have color palettes made up in our heads, I call them inner color palettes. Often, those color palettes change through seasons and as we age.

In fact, most of our behavioral habits and purchases are based on those same inner color palettes.

Why do we do it?

Psychologically, if we match the color from our visions to our physical reality, then our outside world matches our insides. This turns life itself into our inner visions.

Color exists for this exact reason. Color isn't just for dreams. Color has the ability, when used correctly, to turn your own life into one conscious dream.

This book was designed to trigger those inner color palettes and inspire you to dream out loud through color.

Enjoy,

X0X0 Renae Christine
Publisher

SUMMER ENDS WITH SCINTILLATING REDS

AS THE TREES GAIN THEIR AUTUMN HUES.

WARM SCARVES AND LIGHT JACKETS

AS YOU STEP OUT FOR THE EVENING WITH FRIENDS,

EAGER TO LEAVE THE WEEK BEHIND AND TO SEE

WHAT ADVENTURES THE WEEKEND BRINGS.

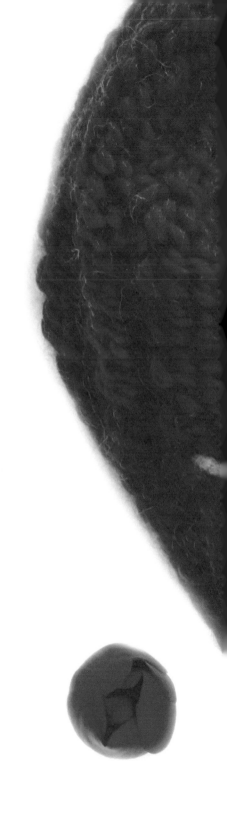

JUICY RED WATERMELON

DRIPPING FROM YOUR CHIN;

STEAMY SCRAMBLED EGGS

CRISPY BACON

AND PERFECTLY SEASONED HOME FRIES...

A PERFECT FARMSTEAD MORNING.

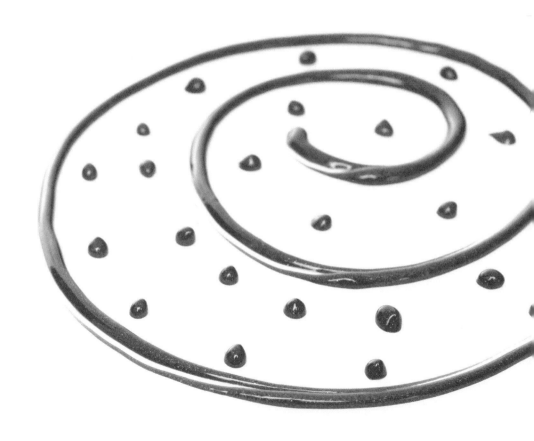

house

SUCCULENT RED RASPBERRIES

PICKED AT THE HEIGHT OF SUMMER.

LUSCIOUS FRUIT JAM SPREAD

ON A LIGHTLY SALTED CRACKER,

THE PERFECT PICNIC SNACK.

FAIRIES PLAY AMONGST THE BRIGHT, ROSY GLADIOLAS

JOINED BY THEIR BEST FRIENDS, AND YOU!

DANCING AROUND THE GARDEN,

BLOOMS TWIRLING WITH THE LIGHT SUMMER BREEZE

THEIR FRANGRANCES, INTOXICATING.

WEARING YOUR SUNDAY BEST,

TEA TIME,

PLAY,

DANCE,

REPEAT!

A TALL TOWER,

A HIDDEN PRINCESS—

WITH ONLY STUFFED TOYS TO KEEP HER COMPANY.

NOT WAITING FOR A PRINCE TO RESCUE HER,

NO,

SHE HAS HER OWN PLANS...

BUBBLES AND FRESH LEMON,

SHINY WHITE PLATES,

A BOWL OF FRESH ORANGES.

SPARKLY COUNTERS

STARTING THE DAY

FRESH.

WARM AUTUMN SUN

WITH A CRISP COOL BREEZE

DANCING AMONG THE FALLEN LEAVES.

SIPPING WARM CIDER,

CLIMBING THE LADDER FOR APPLES

AND ENDING THE DAY WITH

CUDDLING BY AN OUTDOOR FIRE.

A RARE EVENING OUT—

SCINTILLATING SCENTS AND

MOUTHWATERING ENTREES,

CANDLELIGHT AND DESSERT.

A STROLL IN THE MOONLIGHT

A STOLEN KISS UNDER THE STARS.

THE HEIGHT OF SUMMER—

BRILLIANT YELLOW BLOOMS

DOTTING THE GARDEN LANDSCAPE.

A BILLOWING DRESS AS SHE

TWIRLS AND TWIRLS

ONLY TO FALL DOWN,

DIZZY WITH LIFE.

FERNS DANCE MYSTERIOUSLY

IN A BREEZELESS FOREST.

RAIN BOUNCES IN QUICK STACCATOS

ON LOW LYING PLANTS,

WET EARTH AND PETRICHOR.

1.

2.

FAIRY TALES

AND DINOSAURS

ADVENTURES IN THE WILD.

MAGIC AND MYSTERY

WITHOUT LEAVING YOUR BACKYARD.

TOAD STOOLS AND GNOMES,

DASHING SWORDFIGHTS AND

DAMSELS IN DISTRESS;

GOING ANYWHERE AND

EVERYWHERE IN YOUR

IMAGINATION.

SHIVERY WINTER MORNINGS

WRAPPED IN A

SILKY SOFT BLANKET

WITH A HOT CUP OF YOUR

FAVORITE TEA.

THE SCENT OF WOOD DRYING

NEAR THE FIREPLACE,

JUST BROUGHT INSIDE,

DAMP FROM THE

FRESHLY FALLEN SNOW.

A BEACH DAY

PLANTED ON A BLANKET

WITH A GLASS OF

FRESHLY MADE SUN TEA.

WATCHING THE WAVES

GENTLY ROLL TO SHORE

AS KIDS PLAY IN THE SAND,

BUILDING CASTLES AND MOATS

TOES STRETCHED IN THE SAND, THE GRIT

COARSE YET COMFORTING ON YOUR FEET—

THE WARMTH SPREADING

THROUGHOUT YOUR BODY.

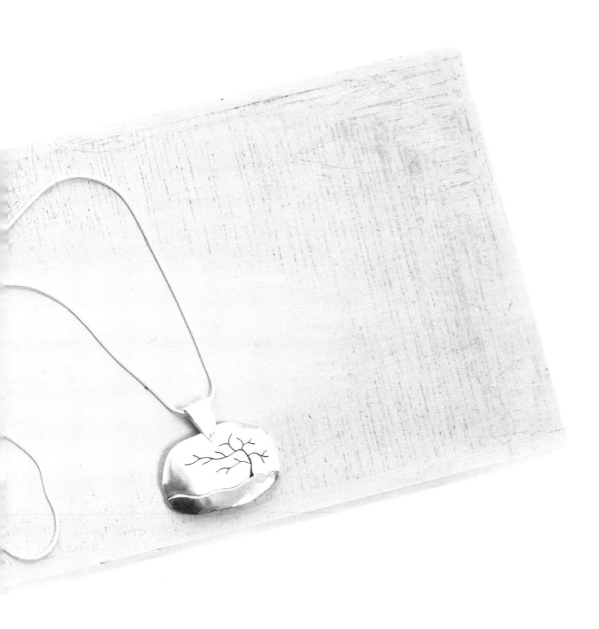

NO MATTER THE DISTANCES

BETWEEN US

FAMILY IS ALWAYS CLOSE BY;

A HANDWRITTEN NOTE,

STEAMING COFFEE IN A FAVORITE MUG

PICTURES ON OUR WALL.

HOME
where the
♥
IS

THE LOVE BETWEEN
Grandma & Madison
KNOWS NO DISTANCE

GRANDMA ♥

PREPARING FOR THE DAY

QUIET AND CALM.

A FAVORITE SILKY MOISTURIZER,

A TOUCH OF POWDER,

A SPRITZ OF YOUR FAVORITE SCENT

BEFORE STEPPING OUT INTO THE MORNING.

FIRST SNOW OF YEAR

SPARKLES AND SHINES

UNDER THE STREET LIGHTS.

SOFT AND TRANQUIL,

THE INCHES GATHER

MAKING THE WORLD FRESH AND NEW.

TRANQUILITY IN THE OCEAN,

IN THE DEEP BLUE

SHIMMERING SUNLIGHT

AGAINST THE SURFACE OF THE WATER

WHERE WHALES SING

AND DOLPHINS FROLIC;

WHERE POSSIBILITY

RESIDES IN THE DEEP.

wherever
we go,
let's go
together

85

LUSCIOUS LAYERS OF TULLE,

PIROUETTES AS SHE DANCES ON STAGE

(FOR HER STUFFED ANIMAL AUDIENCE).

LEAPING, CAUGHT BY THE

HANDSOME PRINCE—

BOWING TO A STANDING OVATION

BEFORE COLLAPSING IN GIGGLES.

RIBBONS AND SWIRLS,

SOARING JUMPS

AND SWEEPING ORCHESTRAL SCORES.

A NEW DREAM BORN

AS SHE WATCHES THE DANCER

SPIN ACROSS THE STAGE.

A COZY FIRE ON A

NOVEMBER AFTERNOON;

SPENDING TIME WITH A

SISTER, BEST FRIEND

PAINTING YOUR NAILS FOR THE WEEK

EXPERIMENTING WITH DEEP WINTER HUES.

WOOD SNAPPING AND CRACKLING

A GLASS (OR TWO) OF MERLOT

LAUGHING AT OLD STORIES,

TOLD A THOUSAND TIMES OVER

AND ADVENTURES OF CHILDHOOD.

SURRENDERING TO THE WARM,

SOOTHING WATERS

SERENITY AND PEACE.

THE NEWEST ISSUE

OF YOUR FAVORITE MAGAZINE

AND FLICKERING CANDLELIGHT

SOOTHING THE LAST VESTIGES

OF A LONG DAY.

DEEP BREATHS AS YOU PREPARE

YOURSELF FOR THE BIG DAY;

HINTS OF SPARKLE,

OPULENT FLOWERS

FAMILY AND FRIENDS

GATHERED IN LOVE.

A DUSKY GRAY EVENING

STARS JUST COMING OUT TO PLAY

AS THE LAST BIT OF SUMMER RAIN

BURNS OFF—

LEAVING BEHIND

TWINKLING WET PAVEMENT

AND RAINDROPS DANCING ON

BLADES OF GRASS AS YOU STEP OUT

FOR A STROLL.

THE SCENT OF WARM CHOCOLATE

FILLING YOUR NOSE.

MUSKY VANILLA

AND GLIMMERING FLAMES,

SILKS AND SATINS

SETTLING IN FOR THE EVENING—

NETFLIX AND YOUR FAVORITE MOVIE.

GEARING THEM UP FOR ADVENTURE—

DESIGNING A ROOM

WITH IMAGES TO INSPIRE

FLIGHTS OF FANCY

AND JOURNEYS

THROUGH A MAGICAL WARDROBE

OR DOWN A RABBIT HOLE

WHERE ANYTHING IS POSSIBLE.

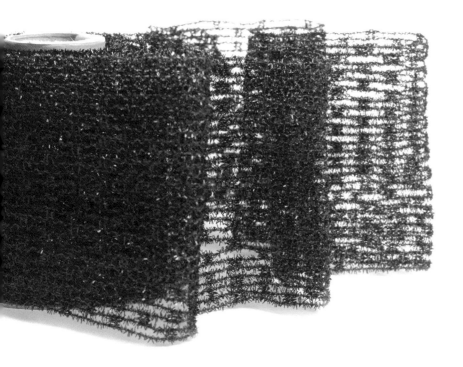

A HOME BUILT IN LOVE

THE KITCHEN AT THE HEART OF IT;

ALWAYS THE GATHERING PLACE

WHEN FRIENDS AND FAMILY

COME TOGETHER

TO CELEBRATE A

MILESTONE OR HOLIDAY

OR MAYBE JUST TWO CLOSE FRIENDS

SIPPING COFFEE IN THE QUIET.

SEA OTTERS HOLD HANDS WHILE SLEEPING SO THEY DON'T DRIFT AWAY FROM EACH OTHER

WHICH PAGES TRIGGERED YOUR INNER COLOR PALETTE?

Match your physical surroundings with
the same colors you gravitated toward
in this book and see what happens.
You may find yourself smiling.

AFTER USE INSTRUCTIONS:

Step 1. Sit quietly and think about your favorite pages.

Step 2. Place book on a coffee table or side table. —You're going to want to open it soon again!

Step 3. Leave a review on Amazon since you're a nice person like that. *Wink

RENAE CHRISTINE

ABOUT THE PUBLISHER

Renae's favorite color combo is white and
different shades of pink, like in pink peonies.

CAREY BUNKER

ABOUT THE AUTHOR

Carey's favorite colors include different shades of turquoise, teal and aqua.

Credits:

Red Silk Clutch
JoanyG
etsy.com/shop/joanyg
p. 15

Cowl
Knitz and Pieces
etsy.com/shop/KnitzAndPieces
p. 15

Watermelon Bowl
Glass Bowls by Katy Jean
glassbowlsbykatyjean.etsy.com
p. 18

Farmhouse Pillow
Sew A Fine Seam
sewafineseam.bigcartel.com
p. 19

Red Ticking Apron
Narley and Chikki
etsy.com/shop/narleyandchikki
p. 18

Chocolate-Dipped Cookies
Tasty Confections
tastyconfections.etsy.com
p. 22

Ceramic Plate
Lost Mountain Pottery
LostMountainPottery.etsy.com
p. 22

Cognac and Vanilla Cherry Jam
LAFG Studio
www.etsy.com/shop/LAFarmGirl
p. 23

Fairy Peg Dolls
Tiffany Lee Studios
tiffanyleestudios.com p. 26

3-D Felt Wall Art
Catshy Crafts
www.etsy.com/shop/catshycrafts
p. 26

Crocheted Animals
Rothwood Row
rothwoodrow.com p. 26, 27

Dance & Play Bracelets
Amy Catherine Designs
amycatherinedesigns.com
p. 30, 31

Flower Clutch
Lolos
etsy.com/shop/lolos p. 30

Beaded Bracelet
Sparkle by Monica
sparklebymonica.com p. 70

Chalkboard
EverArizona
etsy.com/shop/everarizona
p. 34

Pink Mouse
Yeni Stitches
etsy.com/shop/yenistitches
p. 34

Eiffel Tower Bag
Indigo Crane
etsy.com/shop/IndigoCrane
p. 34

Princess Castle Toothfairy Pillow
Handmade Happiness by Ruth
handmadehappinessbyruth.com
p. 35

Flower Blanket
The Dancing Squirrel
thedancingsquirrel.com p.39

Tea Towel
Debbie Tomassi Design
debbietomassidesign.com
p. 39

CPSIA information can be obtained at www.ICGtesting.com
Printed in the USA
LVIW01n0826250617
539294LV00004B/7